The 7 Laws of the Teacher – A Walk Thru the Bible Classic!

A "classic" is something that has been around for a while, is highly esteemed for its value, and has had a long-standing impact in people's lives. With that being the case, *The 7 Laws of the Teacher* certainly qualifies as a classic. For two decades, this teaching series has changed the way teachers and facilitators understand and approach their teaching. And many lives—both students and teachers—have been changed as well!

The 7 Laws of the Teacher, along with the other two titles in the Walk Thru the Bible teaching collection—*The 7 Laws of the Learner* and *Teaching With Style*—has equipped teachers in over 85 countries around the world. Although the look of the video may be a bit dated, the material is just as relevant today as when the series was first introduced by Dr. Howard Hendricks.

The challenges encountered by teachers today are daunting. Teachers are faced with issues like teaching in a world inundated with technology, constant changes in our knowledge base, global and economic information overload, and a multitude of distractions. It's a challenge to be an effective and engaging teacher. Walk Thru the Bible can help!

The 7 Laws of the Teacher is the answer to an age-old question—how to teach so that students learn, retain information, and have passion for learning! We are pleased that you have joined us for a transformational experience. Through this course, you will learn seven essential principles that will forever change the way you approach your teaching and will help your students enjoy learning. Welcome to *The 7 Laws of the Teacher*!

When you've completed this series, be sure to check out the other two modules in our teaching series—*The 7 Laws of the Learner* and *Teaching With Style*. Your teaching will never be the same!

Walk Thru the Bible has been creating teaching and discipleship materials for more than 30 years. These materials have reached millions of people across the globe through live teaching events, print publications, and small group study curricula. Our commitment is to ignite a passion for God's Word and to help people everywhere live His Word.

Learn more about the complete teaching series at www.walkthru.org/teachingseries. Also, check out our DVD series on parenting, family, marriage, personal holiness, as well as our other small group and personal study materials, Bibles, books, and daily devotionals at www.walkthru.org. Or call 1-800-361-6131.

Take a Walk. Change the World.

Copyright © 1988, 2010 by Walk Thru the Bible Ministries, Inc. All rights reserved.

Copyright © 1988, 2010
by Walk Thru the Bible Ministries
All rights reserved.

Published by
Walk Thru the Bible Ministries
4201 North Peachtree Rd., Atlanta, Georgia 30341-1207
www.walkthru.org 1-800-361-6131

Unless otherwise noted, all Scriptures quoted are taken from
The New King James Version, © 1979,1950,1982 by Thomas Nelson, Inc.
Used by permission.

This course workbook is not to be reproduced in any form without written premission from Walk Thru the Bible Ministries.

The 7 Laws of the Teacher Course Workbook

Contents

LAW 1: THE LAW OF THE TEACHER 5

LAW 2: THE LAW OF EDUCATION 15

LAW 3: THE LAW OF ACTIVITY 25

LAW 4: THE LAW OF COMMUNICATION 37

LAW 5: THE LAW OF THE HEART 49

LAW 6: THE LAW OF ENCOURAGEMENT 61

LAW 7: THE LAW OF READINESS 73

NOTES ANSWER KEY 86

DVD Instructor

Dr. Howard Hendricks

The 7 Laws of the Teacher DVD series contains the distilled wisdom of more than four decades of ministry by Dr. Howard G. Hendricks, internationally known as a trailblazing christian educator who practices what he preaches.

The founder and former chairman of the Christian Education department of Dallas Theological Seminary in Dallas, Texas, he now serves as Distinguished Professor and Chairman of the Christian Leadership Center at the Seminary.

Dr. Hendricks has received the AB and DD degrees from Wheaton College and the ThM from Dallas Theological Seminary, where he also studied toward the ThD. He has pursued graduate study at a number of other institutions. For the past four decades he has served in a variety of roles as a professor and pastor. He is a frequent speaker at Christian education conferences and in wide demand for pulpit supply and Bible teaching. He has ministered in more than 70 countiries around the world.

Listed in *Who's Who in American Education*, Dr. Hendricks has served on a number of boards and committees. He has served as a member of the board of directors for Walk Thru the Bible Ministries, The Navigators, Search Ministries, and other organizations.

Dr. Hendricks, a best-selling author, has written *Confrontation, Conflict and Crisis; Say It with Love; Heaven Help the Home; Families Go Better with Love; Marriage and the Family; Church Management Manual; Taking a Stand;* and *Teaching to Change Lives;* he is coauthor with his wife Jeanne of *Footprints: Walking Through the Passages of Life*. He is the founding teacher of "The Art of Family Living," heard on more than 160 radio stations across the U.S.

Howard and Jeanne are the parents of four grown children.

Copyright © 1988, 2010 by Walk Thru the Bible Ministries, Inc. All rights reserved.

How to Use Your Course Workbook

This Course Workbook for *The 7 Laws of the Teacher* will help you derive the most benefit from your DVD sessions with Dr. Howard G. Hendricks. Follow these simple steps:

1. Get your mind in gear as you prepare for the DVD session by reading through the "Thought Joggers," a collection of quotes, anecdotes, and ideas for your consideration.

2. Think through the subject of the session before the DVD presentation begins by using the "Preparing Yourself" page.

3. Follow along with Dr. Hendricks by using the DVD Outline note pages included for each session. There's extra room for you to add your own notes and thoughts.

4. After the DVD outline, you'll find these extra helps:

    - **Let's Talk About It**—Some questions designed to launch small group discussions and help you learn from one another's experience and expertise on the session's subject.

    - **How Am I Doing?**—A self-evaluation to help you to determine how well you are already using the law you've learned in your own teaching situations, and to identify areas in which you need improvement.

    - **Let's Take Action**—Practical application steps you can take in order to begin putting the law you've learned to work immediately as you communicate to others.

    - **On Your Own**—Ideas for further work and study on this law to help you apply it in your own life. After each class session, be sure to review your notes from the DVD and spend some time working through the follow-up sections. If you missed filling in a blank or two, you'll find them in the Notes Answer Key on pages 86-87.

Use this workbook to help you review *The 7 Laws of the Teacher* often, and grow to become a master communicator.

Copyright © 1988, 2010 by Walk Thru the Bible Ministries, Inc. All rights reserved.

Law One
The Teacher
A Ministry of Mediocrity or Multiplication?

Law 1

Thought Joggers

"Not many of you should become teachers. As you know, we teachers will be judged with greater strictness than others."
James 3:1
(GOOD NEWS VERSION)

"In truth you cannot read the Scriptures too much; and what you read, you cannot read too well; and what you read well, you cannot too well understand; and what you understand well, you cannot too well teach; and what you teach well, you cannot too well live."
Martin Luther

"A teacher affects eternity; no one can tell where his influence stops."
Henry Brooks Adams

"I would rather have my student drink from a running stream than from a sagnant pool."
A Professor

Preparing Yourself

Your Enthusiasm Index
Indicate the degree to which each statement below actually describes you in your current (or most recent) teaching situation:

1. I tend to think about my students outside of class.
2. I usually wish the class time was longer.
3. I look forward to finding time to learn more about the subject on my own.
4. My students have told me that I excited their interest in the subject.
5. I often talk with students after (or outside) class.
6. I tend to tell others about my class and students.
7. I have "fun" teaching my class.
8. I usually look forward to my class.
9. I tend to come early to class.
10. I tend to enjoy my preparation time and efforts for class.

Scoring Instructions

Each column heading has an assigned value (4,3,2,1,0). Add the total score value for each of the five categories and then total your overall score in the blank provided. Use this table to measure your EQ-your Enthusiasm Quotient:

35-40 = A
30-34 = B
25-29 = C+
20-24 = C
15-19 = C-
10-14 = D
0-9 = Oops!

HOWARD HENDRICKS / THE 7 LAWS OF THE TEACHER

LAW 1 / THE LAW OF THE TEACHER

	STRONGLY AGREE 4	AGREE 3	UNSURE 2	DISAGREE 1	STRONGLY DISAGREE 0
	____	____	____	____	____
	____	____	____	____	____
	____	____	____	____	____
	____	____	____	____	____
	____	____	____	____	____
	____	____	____	____	____
	____	____	____	____	____
	____	____	____	____	____
	____	____	____	____	____
	____	____	____	____	____
SubTotal	____	____	____	____	____
Total	____	____	____	____	____

Law 1

HOWARD HENDRICKS / THE 7 LAWS OF THE TEACHER

Thought Joggers

"But grow in the grace and knowledge of our Lord and Savior Jesus Christ."
2 Peter 3:18 NIV

"And the things you have heard me say in the presence of many witnesses entrust to reliable men who will also be qualified to teach others."
2 Timothy 2:2 NIV

A doctor's mistake is buried.
A lawyer's mistake is imprisoned.
An accountant's mistake is written off.
A dentist's mistake is pulled.
A plumber's mistake is stopped.
An electrician's mistake is shocked.
A printer's mistake is reprinted.
But a teacher's mistake is never erased.

The Teacher

A Ministry of Mediocrity or Multiplication?
- Definition of the Law of the Teacher
- A Teacher Must Know Two Things
- Three Basic Insights
- Implementing the Truth of This Law
- A Review . . . The Law Applied

I. Definition of the Law of the Teacher

"If you stop _____ today, you stop teaching tomorrow."

II. A Teacher Must Know Two Things

A. Content: What they teach (inculcating principles)

B. Constituents: Whom they teach (infecting people)

III. Three Basic Insights

A. The Law of Teaching embraces a philosophy.

1. "The teacher is primarily a _____."

2. "You cannot impart what you do not _____."

Copyright © 1988, 2010 by Walk Thru the Bible Ministries, Inc. All rights reserved.

LAW 1 / THE LAW OF THE TEACHER

B. The Law of Teaching requires an attitude.

1. "An attitude that you have not _____."

2. "You learn from the past, but you don't _____ in it."

3. "I believe the greatest threat to teaching is _____ because the good is the enemy of the better, and the better is the enemy of the best."

4. The teacher should not assume interest but create it.

5. "Knowledge is proud that it knows so much; Wisdom is _____ because it knows so little."

C. The Law of Teaching involves a relationship.

1. This relationship is a delicate balance between:

   • content and _____

   • facts and _____

   • what you teach and how you teach it.

2. "The nature of the message determines the nature of the _____."

Law 1

Thought Joggers

"The teacher is an informed guide whose knowledge of a given area enables him to direct a learner's efforts to attain wisdom, thus saving the learner's time and strength and helping him discern truth from error."
Amy Magaw

"Whatever you do, don't bore people with the Word of God."

"There cain't nobody teach me who don't know me and won't learn me."
A Student

"Ultimately, what you are is far more important than what you say or what you do."

The Teacher

IV. Implementing the Truth of This Law

A. Have a consistent study and reading program.

- "Readers are _____ and leaders are readers."

Three suggestions:

1. If you have an hour, read for a half hour and reflect for the other half hour.

2. Enroll in continuing education courses.

3. Most important, "you ought to devise a _____ study program."

B. Get to Know Your Students

1. Know their names and needs.

2. _____ over your students.

3. A warning: "I believe when working with people that labels are libel."

Copyright © 1988, 2010 by Walk Thru the Bible Ministries, Inc. All rights reserved.

C. Make an Intensive Personal Evaluation

1. "Experience does not make you better. It tends to make you worse—unless it is _____ experience."

2. *Key Suggestion*: As you walk out of class, ask: "How could I do it _____?"

3. "The greatest threat to your ministry is your ministry—the danger of being so busy *doing* things that you are not *becoming* something significant."

4. "God cannot work through you until He works _____ you."

V. A Review . . . The Law Applied

Law 1

HOWARD HENDRICKS / THE 7 LAWS OF THE TEACHER

Thought Joggers

"It is not until people get into the Word of God for themselves that you begin to see significant, supernatural changes in the lives of those individuals."
Amy Magaw

"Most of us read too much and reflect too little."
Howard Hendricks

Let's Talk About It

1. Based on your understanding of the Scriptures below, what is the role/responsibility of a teacher?
   - "Show me Your ways, O LORD; teach me Your paths. Lead me in Your truth and teach me . . . " (Psalm 25:4-5).
   - "And the things that you have heard from me among many witnesses, commit these to faithful men who will be able to teach others also" (2 Timothy 2:2).
   - "For though by this time you ought to be teachers, you need someone to teach you again the first principles of the oracles of God . . . " (Hebrews 5:12).

2. Read the two descriptions below, then answer the questions.

   > **Teacher A** is a warm, caring individual who is always enthusiastic about the class and plans numerous social events with his students. While his Bible knowledge and teaching skills are mediocre, his class is always popular because of his obvious love for his students and fellowship with them.

   > **Teacher B** is an excellent teacher who has obviously spent many hours (and years!) in preparation. He does not enjoy class fellowships and rarely participates in class/church social events. His class has good attendance because of his Bible teaching, but he maintains little contact with students outside class.

   In whose class would you prefer to be, Teacher A or Teacher B? Why? Which teacher do you more closely resemble?

3. A Chinese proverb notes, "He teaches best who teaches least." If your role as a teacher is to guide discovery, list three or four ways you can help your class into the personal discovery of biblical truth.

4. Identify and discuss an incident in the ministry of Jesus in which He guided His learners into a personal understanding of a principle rather than just "preaching a sermon" to them. (Examples: feeding the 5,000, Matthew 14:13-21; walking on water, Matthew 14:22-33.)

Copyright © 1988, 2010 by Walk Thru the Bible Ministries, Inc. All rights reserved.

LAW 1 / THE LAW OF THE TEACHER

How Am I Doing?

Circle the number representing how accurately the statement reflects you.
1 = always, 2 = usually, 3 = sometimes, 4 = rarely, 5 = never.

1.	I spend time in prayer for each of my students.	1	2	3	4	5
2.	I spend at least two hours preparing for each class.	1	2	3	4	5
3.	I spend time each day in Bible reading and Bible study.	1	2	3	4	5
4.	I vary the activities and methods I use in presenting the Bible context.	1	2	3	4	5
5.	I begin every presentation with clearly-defined goals and objectives.	1	2	3	4	5
6.	I consider my teaching responsibility as a response to a call from God.	1	2	3	4	5
7.	I encourage student participation during the class.	1	2	3	4	5
8.	I regularly provide suggestions/guidelines for further study and applications of the lesson/topic.	1	2	3	4	5
9.	I have defined methods of evaluating whether my students have learned during the lesson/quarter/year.	1	2	3	4	5
10.	I regularly participate in a variety of activities that will enhance my teaching skills (live events, workshops, reading books and magazines, etc.).	1	2	3	4	5

Law 1

HOWARD HENDRICKS / THE 7 LAWS OF THE TEACHER

Thought Joggers

Let's Take Action

At this point in the first lesson, you may be feeling either very good or very bad about yourself as a teacher! This section is designed to help you identify specific areas of change that you would like to make, so that you can become a master teacher.

Based on the information in this lesson, put an X beside those items you would like to strengthen in your own life.

_____ a warm, caring attitude for my class

_____ a proper balance between content and communication

_____ a commitment to continued learning

_____ a wide(r) variety of teaching methods

_____ increased time in prayer and Bible study

_____ an honest evaluation of my teaching skills

_____ a commitment to more thorough preparation for teaching

Now write your initials in the margin by the one item you will honestly and consistently work on in the next week.

On Your Own

Jesus was indeed the Master Teacher. However, He taught without the use of a workbook, DVD, or even a Sunday school curriculum! Moreover, we are told that crowds stayed to listen to Him for long periods of time, so that the disciples expressed concern about their need for food (Matthew 14:15,16). Certainly He is a teacher worthy of our study!

Select a passage in which Jesus is primarily teaching (such as the Sermon on the Mount). Read the passage carefully several times, then answer the following questions:

The passage I studied was _____ in which Jesus taught about _____
_____
_____

His central point was _____
_____
_____

His objective in teaching this was ____
_____
_____
_____

From observing His teaching style here, I learned _____
_____
_____
_____
_____
_____

Copyright © 1988, 2010 by Walk Thru the Bible Ministries, Inc. All rights reserved.

Law Two
Education
What's Left Over After You've Forgotten the Facts

Law 2

Thought Joggers

"Personally I'm always ready to learn, although I do not always like to be taught."
Winston Churchill

"The chief end of education is not to make students dependent upon teachers, but to prepare them to educate themselves throughout their lives."
Amy Magaw

"It is not what is poured into the student, but what is planted there, that counts."
Eugene Bertin

"So that your trust may be in the Lord, I have instructed you today, even you."
Proverbs 22:19

Preparing Yourself

Measuring Your Success

Read each description and check the criterion you feel is most crucial in determining a person's level of success.

The Coach:

A basketball coach is judged to be successful based on:

____ How he/she can shoot baskets.
____ How he/she explains strategy to the players.
____ How his/her team plays basketball.

The Sales Manager:

A sales manager is considered successful if:

____ He/she makes a lot of sales.
____ He/she leads an enjoyable sales staff meeting.
____ His/her sales staff makes a lot of sales.

The Teacher:

A teacher is considered successful when:

____ He/she knows the subject very well.
____ He/she presents an interesting lesson.
____ His/her students know the subject very well.

Copyright © 1988, 2010 by Walk Thru the Bible Ministries, Inc. All rights reserved.

LAW 2 / THE LAW OF EDUCATION

The obvious conclusion . . .

1. Using the case studies above, what generally is the measure of success?

_____

_____

_____

_____

_____

2. As a teacher, where should you focus your efforts in order to succeed?

_____

_____

_____

_____

_____

Law 2

Thought Joggers

"The problem with education today is that most teachers give out fruit rather than plant seeds."

"Though a teacher cannot teach what he does not know, he can inspire students to learn what he does not know."

"You can teach a student a lesson for a day, but if you create curiosity, he will continue to learn as long as he lives."

"Education is what you get from reading the fine print."
Chinese proverb

Education

What's Left Over After You've Forgotten the Facts
- Definition of the Law of Education
- Four Exceptions
- Teaching Goals
- Four Basics

I. Definition of the Law of Education

A. Education is "the process of exciting and directing the

_____ of the pupil."

B. There is the _____ phase ("exciting") and

there is the _____ phase ("directing").

C. The key expression is the *self-activity*.

LAW 2 / THE LAW OF EDUCATION

Clarifying the Roles

The Teacher	The Student
Stimulator	
Motivator	
Coach	

II. Four Exceptions

Special circumstances that may impact the way this law of teaching is applied.

A. When your objective is to save _____.

B. When you are confronted by certain types of students:

   1. The _____ student.

   2. The _____ student.

   3. The _____ student.

   4. The _____ student.

C. When you have intense _____.

D. When you have a _____ individual.

Law 2

Thought Joggers

"As a rule, tell the student nothing that the student can learn for himself."

"The key to education is not what you do, but what the student does."

"The beginning student is a lot like a baby learning to walk. He needs to know that failure is part of the process of learning."

"My primary task is communicating to the student, 'I believe in you. You're going to make it.'"

Education

III. Teaching Goals

Three things students need to learn.

A. Students need to learn how to _____ .

  1. "Your task as a teacher is to stretch the human mind. The human mind is just like a muscle. It develops with usage."

  2. The Parable of the Sower (Mark 4:1-20).

     Only one variable: the soil.

     "The key to the parable is the _____ of the listener."

B. Students need to learn how to _____ .

  1. Learning is always a _____ .

  2. Learning is a _____ process.

  3. Learning is a _____ process.

C. Students need to learn how to _____ in order to develop people who:

  - are self-directed.
  - are disciplined.
  - do what they do because they choose to do it.

LAW 2 / THE LAW OF EDUCATION

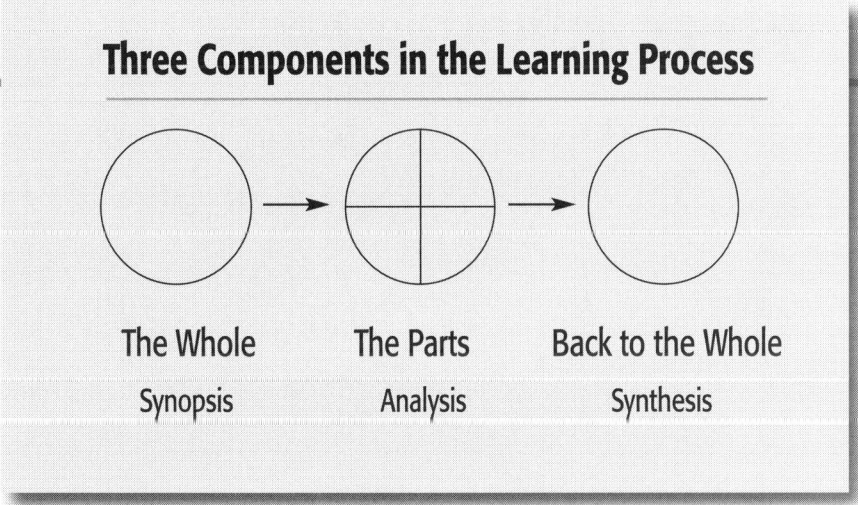

"Never do anything for a student which the student is capable of doing for himself."

"I would suggest you need to spend more time questioning answers rather than answering questions."

IV. Four Basics

A. Teach them to _____.

B. Teach them to _____.

C. Teach them to _____.

D. Teach them to _____.

Law 2

Thought Joggers

"What good is a revelation if you can't read it?"

"If you want to change a person permanently, change his thinking, not his behavior."
Amy Magaw

"Every moment you live, you learn. Every moment you learn, you live."

"Has anybody ever walked out of your class so thirsty that they can hardly wait to get the next drink for themselves?"

HOWARD HENDRICKS / THE 7 LAWS OF THE TEACHER

Let's Talk About It

1. Think back to a lesson or message that you felt "changed your life." List three key points of it below.
   _____
   _____
   _____
   _____

   Was it difficult to list those points? Why? _____
   _____
   _____
   _____
   _____

2. Which is more important: to change a person's thinking, or to change his behavior? Why? _____
   _____

3. Based on the life of Jesus, discuss how He used a "teachable moment" in a specific situation to convey a message.
   Incident: _____
   _____

   Lesson: _____
   _____

4. List three or four questions you could use to stimulate discussion about Nicodemus' visit to Jesus, recounted in John 3.
   _____
   _____
   _____
   _____

Copyright © 1988, 2010 by Walk Thru the Bible Ministries, Inc. All rights reserved.

LAW 2 / THE LAW OF EDUCATION

How Am I Doing?

As a teacher, I agree with the following statements (circle your response):

Yes	No	1. I know my students regularly study their lesson.
Yes	No	2. I have confidence that my students regularly discover new insights in the Bible through my teaching.
Yes	No	3. I am excited about the variety of individual needs my students bring to class.
Yes	No	4. I am sure that I "plant seeds" more often than I "give fruit."
Yes	No	5. I stimulate my students by asking questions instead of always giving answers.
Yes	No	6. My students usually understand when I demonstrate the "whole-parts-whole" principle in Bible teaching.
Yes	No	7. I am interested in changing the thinking of my students as well as their behavior.

Law 2

Thought Joggers

"Truth is always most profitable and most productive when you can see it for yourself."

Let's Take Action

Spend a few minutes reflecting about each student as an individual in your class or learning situation. Select two or three characteristics or needs of each person. In the space below, list the most critical of the needs you have identified:

_____

_____

_____

_____

_____

_____

_____

_____

Spend a few moments in prayer, asking God to help you meet those needs in the next few weeks.

On Your Own

Commit to making a plan to address the most critical needs that you have identified with your students.

_____

_____

_____

_____

_____

_____

_____

_____

_____

_____

Enlist the help of others if necessary to meet these needs.

Make a commitment.

I commit to do the above by:

_____
(Date)

Law Three
Activity
Changing into the Image of Christ

Law 3

Thought Joggers

"People, like trees, must grow or die. There's no standing still. A tree dies when its roots become blocked."

"And just as you want men to do to you, you also do to them likewise."
Jesus in Luke 6:31

"Action may not always bring about learning, but there is no learning without action."
Amy Magaw

Preparing Yourself

Tried and True

Every field of endeavor such as teaching has its axioms and assumptions. Most are founded on fact and proven experience. They help people operate more effectively in their field by providing governing principles of application. Other axioms and assumptions, however, may not be as accurate or appropriate—even though on the surface they may seem on target.

Many beliefs and preconceived notions govern our approach to teaching whether consciously or not. Let's look at several of the more "accepted" statements and evaluate whether or not they are true.

LAW 3 / THE LAW OF ACTIVITY

"Practice makes perfect."	True	False
"If my students are quiet, they must be learning."	True	False
"My students should draw personal applications from the Bible principles I teach, rather than me spoon-feeding them."	True	False
"We learn by doing."	True	False
"The more truths you can pack into the session, the more impact it will have."	True	False
"Doctrine must be preached practically, and duties doctrinally."	True	False
"Experience is the best teacher."	True	False

As you watch the DVD with Dr. Hendricks, listen carefully to the way he deals with some of these axioms. You may be surprised!

Law 3

Thought Joggers

"Activity in learning is never an end in itself. It's always a means to an end."
Howard G. Hendricks

"Whenever you read the word 'hear' in the New Testament, you can always translate it 'do.'"

"The name of the game in Christian education is not knowledge, it's obedience."
Amy Magaw

Activity

Changing into the Image of Christ
- Definition of the Law of Activity
- Six Characteristics of Meaningful Activity
- Choosing the Right Approach to Teaching

I. Definition of the Law of Activity

"Maximum learning is always the result of maximum _____."

A. One condition: "The activity must be meaningful."

B. Evaluating three well-known assumptions.

1. Practice makes perfect.
   No: Practice makes permanent!

2. Experience is the best teacher.
   No: Evaluated experience is the best teacher!

3. We learn by doing.
   No: We learn by doing the right things!

LAW 3 / THE LAW OF ACTIVITY

C. A direct correlation: "The higher your _____ the greater your potential for learning."

D. A Chinese proverb:
"I hear, and I forget;
I see, and I remember;
I do and I _____" . . . and I change.

E. Some statistics about remembering:

1. Hearing only—you remember up to _____ %

2. Hearing and seeing—you remember up to _____ %

3. Hearing, seeing, and doing—you remember up to _____ %

F. Learn what Jesus said about hearing and doing.

- Matthew 13:9

- Luke 6:46,47

- Luke 11:28

- John 14:21

Law 3

Thought Joggers

"You build into [your students'] lives. And then to see them go beyond where you are is true fulfillment."

"You're free to make your choices, but you are not free to escape the consequences."

The feeding of the 5,000: "You want *us* to give them something to eat?!" Matthew 14:13-21

Peter walking on water: "Lord, if it is You, command me to come!" Matthew 14:28

Activity

II. Six Characteristics of Meaningful Activity

A. Meaningful activity provides direction without _____.

"You can't pour [education] in; you've got to draw it out."

B. Meaningful activity lays a constant stress on function and _____.

In other words, "How will the student use this material?"

C. Meaningful activity is planned with a _____.

Everytime you teach, ask yourself:
- "What do I want my students to know?"
- "What do I want them to feel?"
- "What do I want them to do?"

D. Meaningful activity concerns itself with the _____ as well as the product.

You have two options:

1. "If you *only* give students a 'product,' then you limit your students by your own _____."

2. "You want to give them a 'process,' because then you launch them on a path with _____ limitations."

Copyright © 1988, 2010 by Walk Thru the Bible Ministries, Inc. All rights reserved.

E. Meaningful activity is _____ and lifelike.

- In other words, similar to what the student will actually face.

F. Meaningful activity involves problem-_____ situations.

"A teacher is a patient person who understands that concepts are built like the layers of an onion. You often have to strip off erroneous ideas that way, and you replace them line upon line, precept upon precept."

Two biblical illustrations of problem-solving situations:

Illustration I: Feeding of the 5,000

Illustration II: Walking on the water

III. Choosing the Right Approach to Teaching.

A. *Option 1:* Produce a _____.

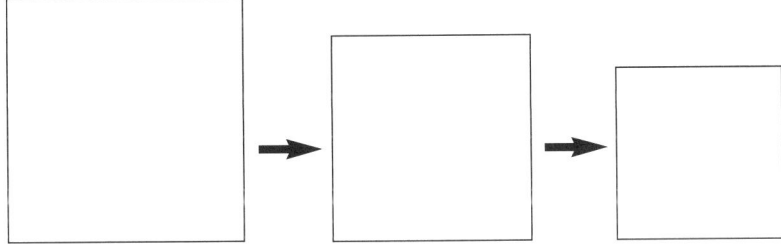

Law 3

Thought Joggers

"You can never share all that you have received. There is always leakage in the process."

Activity

B. *Option 2:* Teach the _____.

- You don't have leakage; you have _____.

- You don't have deterioration; you have dynamic.

C. "Which road are you going to take? I hope you choose wisely."

One Final Recommendation

Study the life of the Savior, the greatest Teacher, and ask, "How did He do it? Did He cram a lot of heads full of a collection of theological facts? Or did He involve them in the process so that the pagan world was compelled to testify, 'These are they who have turned the world upside down?' That's the challenge of Christian education today.

LAW 3 / THE LAW OF ACTIVITY

Let's Talk About It

The following narratives are designed to help you apply the principles of this lesson in typical teaching situations. Use the characteristics of meaningful learning activities as the basis for your discussion.

As a group, choose one (or more) of these narratives and discuss ways that meaningful learning activities could become a vital part of improving teacher effectiveness.

1 Mike and Jan recently moved to a new area and joined First Church. Because of their interest in young people, they are now leading an evening Bible study group. The group has grown steadily over the past few weeks, but it has become more of a social group than a Bible study group. Discuss two or three learning activities that Mike and Jan could use to help the group focus on John 13:14-15 as they continue their study, "How a Young Person Can Walk with Christ."

2 Mrs. Smith loves working with 10-year-old girls. In fact, she has worked with this age group for 17 years. She studies daily and is always excited about her time with the class. She likes crafts and usually has an art project ready for each lesson. Unfortunately, the art project rarely supports any point in the Bible lesson. Mrs. Smith's class, however, consistently has a good time—and all the girls love her. Discuss how Mrs. Smith could use her interest in crafts to teach a lesson based on Matthew 13:3-9.

3 Mr. Adams is one of the mainstays of the Adult Department, having taught for more years than most can remember. His lectures are informative though a bit dull. Identify and discuss two or three learning activities that Mr. Adams could use to increase the effectiveness of his teaching as the class studies Psalm 23.

Law 3

How Am I Doing?

Reflect on the last lesson you taught for a few moments, then place an X on the appropriate line:

____ I think my class had fun, but they probably did not learn much.

____ I am not sure they enjoyed the activities, but at least they behaved!

____ I think they enjoyed the activities, and they probably learned something as well.

____ I am sure that they learned the key points I wanted them to know, and my learning activities supported the Bible teaching.

____ I am not sure what happened!

Based on your answer, how would you evaluate your use of learning activities?

_____
_____
_____
_____
_____
_____

Let's Take Action

A meaningful learning activity does not always involve only physical activity. It may involve mental, emotional, or spiritual activity as well. List an example of each of these that might occur as you study the parable of the Prodigal Son (Luke 15:11-32).

Mental Activity:
_____
_____
_____
_____

Emotional Activity:
_____
_____
_____
_____

Spiritual Activity:
_____
_____
_____
_____
_____

Reflect on the kind of activities that usually take place in your class. Spend a few minutes in prayer, asking God to help you select activities that will meet the varied needs of your class members.

LAW 3 / THE LAW OF ACTIVITY

On Your Own

The following exercise is designed to help you plan a meaningful learning activity for your students. Even though this may not be exactly what you will do in the actual teaching period, it will help you begin to plan ways to make your teaching more exciting for you and your students. Use the sample sheet below to plan at least two activities you will teach. You may use activities suggested in your own teaching materials, refer to your notes or other aids, or include ideas you have developed on your own.

Before you choose an activity, ask yourself these questions:
- What will my students learn from doing this activity?
- How will this activity involve them in learning and applying biblical truth?
- Is the activity appropriate for the interests and age of my students?
- What do I need to do in order to guide this activity?

Learning Activity Planning Sheet

Lesson Title _____
Scripture Studied _____
Lesson Objective _____
List 5-8 possible activities that could be used to support the Scripture lesson:
_____
_____

Answer the following questions about each activity (use another sheet if needed). After this evaluation, you will be able to select the activities you could probably use in teaching the lesson.

Supplies needed _____
Procedures to be used _____
Questions that support the lesson _____
Contributions to the lesson objective _____

As you provide the information for each activity, you will begin to see that some of the activities you considered may not be suitable for your class—some require too many supplies, others may not be suitable for the age group, others may be too time consuming, or you may not be familiar enough with the procedures necessary to use an activity successfully. These observations may not be apparent, however, until you have thought through each one thoroughly. The time spent in this evaluation will be well spent!

Law Four
Communication
An Eight-Stage Model for Teachers

Law 4

Thought Joggers

"Righteous lips are the delight of kings, and they love him who speaks what is right."
Proverbs 16:13

"Communication is a two-way street, but it's often used only for outgoing traffic."

"Impression without expression leads to depression."

"Pray as if it all depended on God. Work as if it all depended on you."

HOWARD HENDRICKS / THE 7 LAWS OF THE TEACHER

Preparing Yourself

Communication or Confusion?

> Bob
> Meet me for lunch . . .
>   Mary

11:35 a.m.
Bob finds a note on his desk.
Mary Smith happens to be out of the office.
Bob sits and ponders his options . . .

How many possible areas of confusion could there be with this "communication"? List them below:

_____
_____
_____
_____
_____

Copyright © 1988, 2010 by Walk Thru the Bible Ministries, Inc. All rights reserved.

LAW 4 / THE LAW OF COMMUNICATION

Apply what you've realized here to your communication as a teacher. What principles or questions come to your mind concerning teaching as a result of this brief exercise? List them below:

_____
_____
_____
_____
_____
_____

The verb *communicate* comes from a Latin word meaning "to make common," and thus "to impart, share, pass along, transmit." How many words can you think of that start with *commun-* ? (There are more than a dozen in the dictionary!) Without looking them up, how would you define them in light of the meaning of the Latin root?

_____
_____
_____
_____
_____
_____

Law 4

Thought Joggers

"Those who minister to others must have something to say—a message that speaks to the need of the hour."

"When it comes to communication, don't assume anything. Just try to explain to someone how to put a coat on without looking!"

"If you know something thoroughly (concept), and if you feel something deeply (feeling), and if you are doing something consistently (action), then you have great potential for being an excellent communicator."

Communication

> **An Eight-Stage Model for Teachers**
> - Introduction
> - Definition of the Law of Communications
> - An Eight-Stage Model of Communications
> - Conclusion

I. Introduction: It's More Difficult Than It Looks

II. Definition of the Law of Communication

A. "Communication . . . is the reason for our existence. It's our business. And don't forget what business you are in."

B. "Communication" comes from the Latin word *communis* meaning _____.

III. An Eight-Stage Model of Communication

A. **Stage 1: Three Essential Components**

1. Concept: Intellectual component.
2. Feeling: Emotional component.
3. Action: Volitional component.

LAW 4 / THE LAW OF COMMUNICATION

B. Stage 2: Words—Communication Symbols

1. "We think it is a word message that we are trying to communicate, and it is not. It is a _____ message."

2. Two essential forms of communication:

    a. Verbal: Two Forms

    - **Speaking**

        Advantages: _____
        _____
        _____
        _____

        Disadvantages: _____
        _____
        _____
        _____

    - **Writing** (also audio, video)

        b. Nonverbal

        "These two forms (verbal and nonverbal) must be congruent. That is, what you say must correspond with what _____ _____."

Law 4

Thought Joggers

"Some people have a built-in radar screen to sense how you feel."

"You need a conclusion. I don't know how many times I've heard a preacher come to the end and circle the field looking for a runway to put that baby down."

Communication

- Research on communication by Albert Mehrabian, Yale University:
  How we communicate:
  Words alone _____ %
  Tone of voice _____ %
  Body language _____ %

Key Question: "Is it more important to witness (i.e., communicate) by my lips (verbally) or by my life (nonverbally)?"
Answer: Both!

C. Stage 3: Speech

1. Preparation

   "You need some structure; you need to _____ your material."

   a. Introduction: Begin with a quotation, question, or problem right out of their life that hooks them.

   b. Conclusion: "The least-prepared part of most messages."

   c. Illustrations: "The _____ that let in the light."

LAW 4 / THE LAW OF COMMUNICATION

2. Presentation

   Three things . . .

   a. _____: Speak clearly

   b. _____: Vary volume, pitch and speed.

   c. _____: "The secret to good gestures is . . . getting it in the gut."

D. Stage 4: Distractions

Two forms . . .
1. Those within the _____ (i.e., those you cannot control).
Examples: attitudes, lack of sleep, illness, other circumstances

2. Those within the _____ (i.e., those you can control).
Examples: temperature of the room, arrangement of the room, materials you will use

> "Up to this point in the process, the focus has been on what **you** do. But beginning at this point, we will focus on what **they** do."

Law 4

Thought Joggers

"Every time you teach or preach, somebody sweats—either you do before or they do during."

"Behind every smile there is a set of teeth."

Communication

E. Stage 5: Listening

1. *Problem*: "The average person can listen from _____ to _____ times as fast as anyone can speak."

2. *Solution*: "You need to combine your speaking with visualization so that they can see what they hear. That's why you use illustrations and analogies."

F. Stage 6: Translation

1. *Problem*: The words that are heard are often different from the words that are sent.

2. *Solution*: They must be allowed to translate them (i.e., make them their own).

G. Stage 7: Three Essential Components

"It's not, 'what do you [the teacher] think?' It's, 'what does he [the student] _____?'

"It's not, 'what do you feel?' "It's, 'what does she _____?'

"It's not, 'what are you doing?' but, 'what are they?' _____? That's the test of communication."

H. Stage 8: Feedback

1. Ask: "Tell me how you can apply this in your sphere of influence."

2. Ask for questions. "They will ask the most perceptive questions to show that you have not put what you want them to know, to feel, to do in a form that they can _____ _____."

Eight Stages of Communication

Your Part "Sender"				Their Part "Receiver"			
Stage 1	**Stage 2**	**Stage 3**	**Stage 4**	**Stage 5**	**Stage 6**	**Stage 7**	**Stage 8**
3 Essential Components	Words	Speech	Distractions	Listening	Translation	3 Essential Components	Feedback
Concept Feeling Action	Verbal Writing	Preparedness Presentation	Controllable Uncontrollable			Students' Thinking Feeling Doing	Application Understanding

IV. Conclusion

"The purpose of communication is not to impress, it's to impart. The purpose of communication is not simply to convince, but to change. Most people communicating, whether it's in the pulpit or in a Bible study class, are focused on the wrong end of the process. They are focusing upon what they are doing as a communicator, as a sender, rather than on what the student, the receptor, is doing."

Law 4

Thought Joggers

"Notice where all of this leads. Our process begins with a concept, feeling, and action, and it ends with a concept, feeling, and action."

Let's Talk About It

1. "Communication" is a big word with lots of meaning. Take a moment to list eight to ten ways of communicating the message, "It's time to eat."
   _____
   _____
   _____

2. Dr. Hendricks identified intellectual, emotional, and volitional components of communication. Beside the statements below, indicate which type of component each one is by writing "I," "E," or "V" in the spaces provided.

   ___ I wish I had more time!
   ___ I am sure the Bible is true.
   ___ I am bothered by his lack of concern.
   ___ I would like to tour the Holy Land.
   ___ I am so happy about your decision to join our group.
   ___ I think your comments about the topic were exactly right.

3. Why is it especially important for the Christian teacher to *say* the same things the students *see* in his life? Can you think of an example in your life in which those are not congruent?
   _____
   _____
   _____

4. Aside from Jesus Christ, who in your opinion is the best communicator in the Bible? Why? What lessons can you learn from that person?
   _____
   _____
   _____

LAW 4 / THE LAW OF COMMUNICATION

How Am I Doing?

Let's examine some of the most common problems in communication. Put a checkmark by those that bother you most.

- ☐ information not complete
- ☐ information too early
- ☐ information too late
- ☐ information intended for someone else
- ☐ confusing information
- ☐ information given too often

Think about the information you have given to your class in the past several weeks. Does it fit in one (or more!) of these categories? What can you do to improve your communication with your students?

_____
_____
_____
_____
_____

Let's Take Action

Here are 12 suggestions for improving your use of language in your communication ministries. Write your initials by at least three that you intend to do in the next 30 days:

____ Read a book on communication.

____ Purchase a book of pithy quotations.

____ Look up the meanings of five words you're not familiar with.

____ Read a literary "classic."

____ Write something worth reading and submit it to a magazine.

____ Spend 15 minutes sitting on the floor talking to a 5-year-old.

____ Spend an hour talking with someone over 75 years old.

____ Read the Book of Acts in a translation or paraphrase you've never used before.

____ Make up a story and tell it to a group of children.

____ Record yourself teaching or in conversation, then listen to find one way you can improve.

Law 4

On Your Own

The words below all convey an aspect of communication:

accept	decide	listen	read	take
admit	direct	look	record	talk
ask	discourage	look up	rejoice	talk with
choose	encourage	love	respond	telephone
commit	evaluate	meet	select	thank
compliment	find	memorize	share	think
confess	give	plan	show	understand
count	help	praise	sing	watch
create	list	pray	study	write

Select at least five words from this list and complete the following sentences using them as the verbs:

I will _____

I will _____

I will _____

I will _____

I will _____

Law Five
Heart
The Essence of Expression and Persuasion

Law 5

Thought Joggers

"Blessed are the pure in heart, for they shall see God."
Matthew 5:8

Jesus in the first of all the commandments is 'Hear, O Israel, the LORD our God, the LORD is one. And you shall love the LORD your God with all your heart, with all your soul, with all your mind, and with all your strength.' This is the first commandment. And the second, like it, is this: 'You shall love your neighbor as yourself.' There is no other commandment greater than these."
Jesus in Mark 12:29-31

"If you would be loved, love and be lovable."
Benjamin Franklin

HOWARD HENDRICKS / THE 7 LAWS OF THE TEACHER

Preparing Yourself

Getting to the Heart of the Matter

1. How would you "subjectively" estimate the degree of "involvement" you have with your students outside of class? Using this scale, color in up to the point that most accurately describes your involvement level.

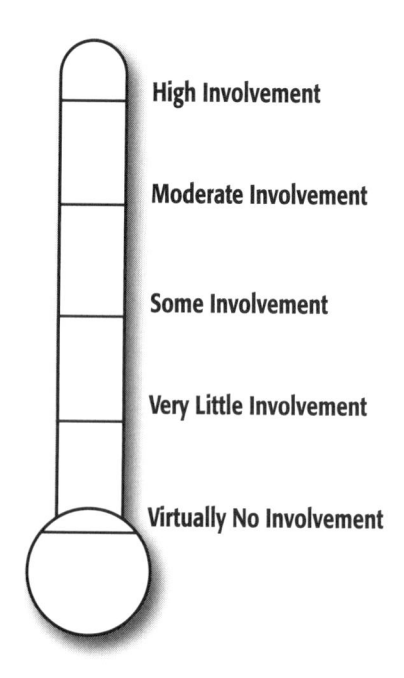

- High Involvement
- Moderate Involvement
- Some Involvement
- Very Little Involvement
- Virtually No Involvement

Copyright © 1988, 2010 by Walk Thru the Bible Ministries, Inc. All rights reserved.

LAW 5 / THE LAW OF THE HEART

2. Which is the more important element of meaningful involvement with your students: quality time or quantity of time? Why?

_____
_____
_____
_____
_____
_____
_____
_____

3. List some of the factors that hinder your being more effectively involved with your students:

_____
_____
_____
_____
_____
_____
_____
_____

Law 5

Thought Joggers

"My soul is too glad and too great to be at heart the enemy of any man."
Martin Luther

"The greatest happiness of life is the conviction that we are loved, loved for ourselves or rather in spite of ourselves."
Victor Hugo

"A good rule for going through life is to keep the heart a little softer than the head."
Kiplinger's Personal Finance

Heart

The Essence of Expression and Persuasion
- Definition of the Law of the Heart
- The Knowing Component
- The Feeling Component
- The Action Component
- Putting It into Practice

I. Definition of the Law of the Heart

"The teaching that impacts is not from head to head, but from heart to _____."

A. The biblical meaning of "heart."

"We need to understand that the Jews used the term 'heart' to embrace the _____ of human personality."

It included:

One's intellect.
One's emotions.
One's will.

B. Socrates' three concepts summarizing the essence of expression and persuasion:

LAW 5 / THE LAW OF THE HEART

1. *"Ethos"* involves _____
   Establishes credentials and credibility of the teacher.

2. *"Pathos"* involves _____
   Involves arousing the passions and massaging the emotions.

3. *"Logos"* involves _____
   Gives understanding and engages the mind.

The Teaching-Learning Process

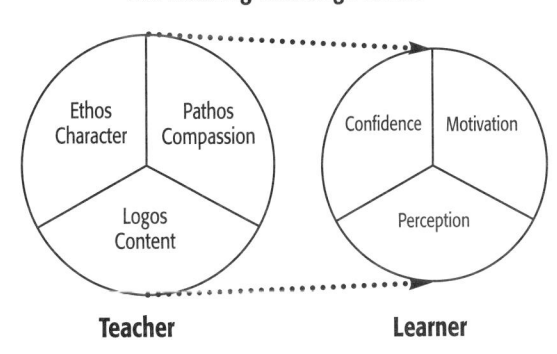

Teacher: Ethos/Character, Pathos/Compassion, Logos/Content

Learner: Confidence, Motivation, Perception

C. How these concepts relate to the learner:

1. The component of character produces _____.

   "The basis of all effective communication emanates from within. And you need to ask yourself periodically the question, 'What kind of person am I?'"

2. The component of compassion produces _____.

3. The component of content produces perception.

Law 5

Thought Joggers

"Hear, O Israel: The LORD our God, the LORD is one! You shall love the LORD your God with all your heart, with all your soul, and with all your strength. And these words which I command you today shall be in your heart."
Deuteronomy 6:4-6

"The focus in teaching is primarily upon what you do. The focus in learning is primarily upon what the student does. Therefore, you test the teaching not by what you do, but by what the student does as a result of what you do."

"When God wanted to communicate with us, He wrapped His message in a Person. And this is exactly what we are called to do."

Heart

D. Relationship between teaching and learning:

Teaching	Learning
Teaching is _____ people to learn.	Learning is essentially producing _____.
Teaching is what _____ do.	Learning is what _____ do.

II. The Knowing Component

A. "Your primary task as a teacher is to perpetuate the _____ process."

B. "You cannot behave correctly unless you believe correctly."

C. Are you dying or developing?

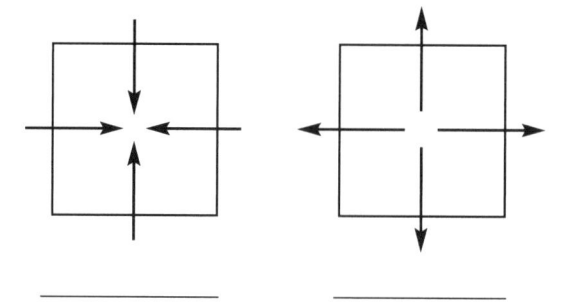

_____   _____

LAW 5 / THE LAW OF THE HEART

III. The Feeling Component

　　A. How it works (2 Corinthians 5:17).

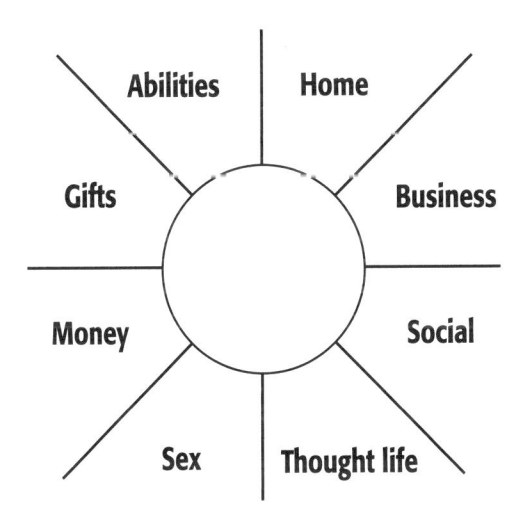

```
        Abilities    Home
   Gifts                  Business
   Money                  Social
        Sex      Thought life
```

　　B. Perspectives that will transform your teaching.

　　　　1. "All learning begins at the _____ level."

　　　　　　If the student has strong negative feelings toward the teacher, he or she will never learn.

　　　　2. People do not care what you know until they know that you _____.

Law 5

Thought Joggers

Mrs. Simpson kept "developing." She went to the Holy Land at age 83 with a group of NFL football players! The night before she died, she wrote out her goals for the next 10 years.

"Therefore, if anyone is in Christ, he is a new creation . . . "
2 Corinthians 5:17

What in the world are you doing "under the circumstances"?

Heart

IV. The Action Component

    A. "This involves changing the things that you are doing

       _____."

    B. "The opposite of ignorance in the spiritual realm is not knowledge.

       It's _____."

V. Putting It into Practice

Four suggestions . . .

    A. Know your students

       1. "It is impossible to meet needs unless you _____ them."

       2. "Sometimes you need to hurt in order to _____."

    B. Earn the right to be their teacher.

       Credibility always precedes _____.

C. Get personally involved with your students.

   "You can impress people at a distance; you can only

   _____ them up close."

D. Become vulnerable before your students.

   "Let them know what you are _____ with."

> "The teaching that impacts is not from head to head. It's from heart to heart. It's a total personality, transformed by the supernatural grace of God, reaching out to transform total personalities by the same grace. What a privilege!"

Law 5

Thought Joggers

"There's a high price tag to good teaching, and it's not available in a bargain basement sale. You've got to be willing to pour your life out like a drink offering."
Amy Magaw

"The closer I am to my students, the greater and the more permanent is the impact."

Let's Talk About It

1. The biblical meaning of "heart" included one's intellect, emotions, and will. What is our role as a teacher in helping our students develop a heart for God?

2. *True or false*: "If the student has not learned, the teacher has not taught." Why did you answer the way you did?

3. Based on your understanding of the importance of *ethos* (confidence), *pathos* (motivation), and *logos* (perception), discuss how these could be applied in a study of Psalm 23.

4. Discuss an example from the teaching ministry of Jesus that supports the statement that the opposite of spiritual ignorance is obedience.

LAW 5 / THE LAW OF THE HEART

How Am I Doing?

You have now reached the fifth session in this series, and you've had several opportunities to evaluate yourself and your teaching style. Here is an opportunity for you to measure your growth during this series. Check your response.

	VERY LITTLE	SOMEWHAT	VERY MUCH
1. I have been faithful in my desire to become more like Jesus, the Master Teacher.	☐	☐	☐
2. I have done outside reading or study between sessions.	☐	☐	☐
3. I have talked with my class about participating in this series on teaching.	☐	☐	☐
4. I have incorporated some of the principles I've learned in teaching my class.	☐	☐	☐
5. I am making changes in my teaching style because I am trying some of the suggested activities.	☐	☐	☐
6. I am spending more time in better preparation each week for my class.	☐	☐	☐
7. I have had feedback from my class about changes they have observed in my teaching as a result of what I've learned and applied from this series.	☐	☐	☐

Law 5

Let's Take Action

These verses are just a small sample of those that deal with the heart. Read them meditatively:

> "I will praise the LORD with my whole heart" (Psalm 111:1).

> "As in water face reflects face, so a man's heart reveals the man" (Proverbs 27:19).

> "Cast away from you all the transgressions which you have committed, and get yourselves a new heart and a new spirit" (Ezekiel 18:31).

> "Let not your heart be troubled; you believe in God, believe also in Me" (John 14:1).

As you think about the intellect, emotions, and will that make up what the Bible calls the heart, select a verse from those above that is especially meaningful to you. In the spaces below, write a sentence or two about how this verse can help you improve your teaching.

_____
_____
_____

During the next week, review this verse daily and commit it to heart.

On Your Own

A fundamental characteristic of a master teacher is knowledge of his or her students. The questions below can be used to help you learn more about your class. Select those that are appropriate for your class situation, then develop a form that you will use with your students.

- Name, address, telephone number
- School, job, title (for adult classes)
- Family members
- Hobbies
- Concerns, needs, prayer requests
- Testimony about Christian life
- Favorite Bible verse/passage
- Favorite motto or wise saying
- Favorite activities in the church
- Interests/abilities useful in class (e.g., plays piano)
- Interesting experiences, trips, etc.

Law Six
Encouragement
The Secrets of Motivating Your Students

Law 6

Thought Joggers

"One of the reasons adults stop learning is that they become less and less willing to risk failure."

"A pat on the back, though only a few vertebrae removed from a kick in the pants, is miles ahead in results."

Preparing Yourself

A Matter of Interest:
Reflecting on your current (or most recent) teaching situation, list at least five specific "motivators" that encourage the interest of your students in learning and applying the principles taught in your class. Then, in the column to the right, indicate whether each motivator is an external (i.e., extrinsic) or internal (i.e., intrinsic) motivator.

	External	Internal
1.	☐	☐
2.	☐	☐
3.	☐	☐
4.	☐	☐
5.	☐	☐
6.	☐	☐
7.	☐	☐
8.	☐	☐
9.	☐	☐

Which type of motivator do you feel is more effective: intrinsic or extrinsic? Why?

Law 6

Thought Joggers

"Confidence is the feeling you have just before you fully understand the situation."

"The mediocre teacher tells. The good teacher explains. The great teacher demonstrates. The superior teacher inspires."
— William Arthur Ward

"A great teacher has always been measured by the number of students who have surpassed him."
— James Hilton

Encouragement

> **The Secrets of Motivating Your Students**
> - Introduction
> - Definition of the Law of Encouragement
> - The Secrets of Motivation
> - Tools for Your Motivational Toolbox
> - One Final Statement

I. Introduction

"It is far more important to determine a person's MQ than their IQ—their Motivational Quotient rather than their Intelligence Quotient."

II. Definition of the Law of Encouragement

A. The Law of Encouragement:

"Teaching tends to be most effective when the student is properly _____."

B. A Motive:

1. "A motive is primarily that within an individual (not without) which causes him to _____."

LAW 6 / THE LAW OF ENCOURAGEMENT

2. Two primary means of motivation:

   a. Extrinsic (i.e., external) motivation

   "Any form of motivation that emanates from _____."

   b. Intrinsic (i.e., internal) motivation

   "Motivation that emanates from _____."

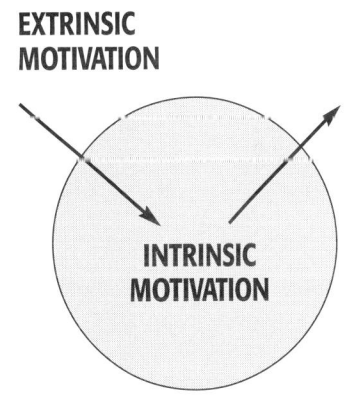

   - "What we are trying to do as a teacher, as a motivator, is to develop a person into a self-starter."

   - "As a teacher, the only place you can work is _____ of the student."

   - "Therefore, the test of all extrinsic motivation is, does it trigger intrinsic motivation? And if it does not, then it is not legitimate."

Law 6

Thought Joggers

"The number one problem in education today is the problem of motivation—overcoming initial inertia, getting the student off the dime and into action."

"I think the reason why God has used me is that, by His grace, the Holy Spirit has developed in me incurable confidence in His ability to change people."
Howard Hendricks

Encouragement

III. The Secrets of Motivation

What do these things tell you about motivation?

• A Book on Baby Care

• A Bible Memory Packet

• A Tax Document

• Merit Badges on a Shirt

IV. Tools for Your Motivational Toolbox

How can I do it? . . .

A. By creating a need.

   1. Two kinds of needs . . .

      a. _____ needs (conscious level)

      b. _____ needs (subconscious level)

LAW 6 / THE LAW OF ENCOURAGEMENT

"Your task as a teacher is to take these real needs and surface them . . .

so that they become felt needs."

Two means by which you can accomplish that:

1. By the _____

2. By _____

B. By developing responsibility with _____ .

"The greater the investment, the greater the interest."

C. By structuring _____ .

Law 6

Thought Joggers

"Every tomorrow has two handles: the handle of anxiety and the handle of faith. Woe to the person who grabs hold of tomorrow by the wrong handle."
— Lawrence B. Casey

Encouragement

Four Major Stages of Training

Hear	See		Do

D. By intensifying _____ relationships

E. By providing recognition and _____.

> "What the Spirit of God would like to do is to use you as His motivational tool working externally to the pupil while He is working internally."

V. One Final Statement

"Everyone can be motivated. But not at the same time. The timing is very crucial. You need a lot of patience to be a good teacher." The investment may take some time but the outcome will be worth it.

LAW 6 / THE LAW OF ENCOURAGEMENT

Let's Talk About It

1. Based on your understanding of the needs of your class, list three to four intrinsic and extrinsic factors that you feel could act as motivators.

Intrinsic	Extrinsic
_____	_____
_____	_____
_____	_____
_____	_____

2. Discuss how a teacher can help meet both felt (conscious) and real (subconscious) needs in a class.

   _____
   _____
   _____
   _____

3. Within your small group, decide on four to six items that could be appropriate in a "motivational toolbox" for one of the following groups:

   - Class of 6 to 8 year-olds

   - Class for married young women

   - Group for married couples

   - "Senior saints" Bible study/fellowship group

   - After-church meeting of youth group

Law 6

HOWARD HENDRICKS / THE 7 LAWS OF THE TEACHER

How Am I Doing?

Reflect for a few moments about some of the people who have encouraged you in the past. List the action or language that you associate with their encouragement.

Action	Language
_____	_____
_____	_____
_____	_____
_____	_____
_____	_____

List three to five ways you have encouraged others in the past week:
_____
_____
_____
_____
_____

How easy was it for you to list those encouraging acts? Why?
_____
_____
_____
_____
_____
_____

Copyright © 1988, 2010 by Walk Thru the Bible Ministries, Inc. All rights reserved.

LAW 6 / THE LAW OF ENCOURAGEMENT

Let's Take Action

You are teaching a series on "How to Study Your Bible," and you quickly discover two disturbing facts: No one in the class knows how, and seemingly no one wants to know how! You think back to some of the tidbits you heard at a recent seminar: "Show them how to do it, let them try it on their own, get them excited about the process (regardless of what the product of their efforts looks like at first), affirm them ('See, you *can* do it!'), and help them evaluate their progress ('Would you like to know how to make it better?')." Suddenly you begin to get excited about the class. You sense this group *can* be motivated to learn how to study the Bible. And you write down five specific action steps that you will follow as you teach the class. Namely:

1. I will _____

2. I will _____

3. I will _____

4. I will _____

5. I will _____

On Your Own

In the space below, list those items you have in your own motivational toolbox. Briefly describe why each is included.

_____

_____

_____

_____

_____

_____

_____

_____

_____

_____

_____

_____

_____

_____

Law 6

Law Seven
Readiness
Necessary Preparation for Maximum Profit

Law 7

Thought Joggers

"If at first you don't succeed, that makes you just about normal."

"The landscape of learning seldom yields its fruit in a single inspection."

Preparing Yourself

Getting a Head Start: Let's think for a moment . . .

1. As a teacher, what steps should you take to prepare for a class?

   _____
   _____
   _____
   _____
   _____
   _____
   _____
   _____
   _____

2. To what degree does your level of preparation affect the quality of your teaching?

   _____
   _____
   _____
   _____
   _____
   _____
   _____
   _____
   _____

LAW # / THE LAW OF READINESS

3. If preparation for the teacher is the key to quality teaching, what is the role of preparation for your students in achieving quality learning?

_____
_____
_____
_____
_____
_____
_____
_____
_____
_____

4. To what degree are your students usually "prepared" for your class in order to maximize their learning experience? _____%
What steps could you take to improve that figure?

_____
_____
_____
_____
_____
_____
_____
_____
_____
_____

Copyright © 1988, 2010 by Walk Thru the Bible Ministries, Inc. All rights reserved.

Law 7

Thought Joggers

"What we need is a flexible plan for an ever-changing world."

"Motivation is what gets you started. Habit is what keeps you going."

"Students are always motivated by at least two reasons: the reason they tell you and the real reason."

"Preach the word! Be ready in season and out of season. Concentrate, rebuke, exhort, with all longsuffering and teaching."
2 Timothy 4:2

HOWARD HENDRICKS / THE 7 LAWS OF THE TEACHER

Readiness

Necessary Preparation for Maximum Profit
- Definition of the Law of Readiness
- The Problem: Students Coming to Class Cold
- The Value of Assignments
- The Characteristics of Good Assignments
- Four Problems in Applying this Law
- Wrapping Up the Series

I. Definition of the Law of Readiness

"Learning tends to be most effective when the student is adequately _____."

II. The Problem: Students Coming to Class Cold

You have two options:

Option 1: Start building interest and understanding at the beginning of class.

Option 2: Start building interest and momentum *before* the class starts.

III. The Value of Assignments

A. They precipitate _____.

B. They provide a background, a _____ on which to build.

C. They develop habits of _____ study.

Copyright © 1988, 2010 by Walk Thru the Bible Ministries, Inc. All rights reserved.

LAW 7 / THE LAW OF READINESS

"The higher your predictability, the lower your impact. Conversely, the lower your predictability, the higher your impact."

IV. The Characteristics of Good Assignments

A. Good assignments must be _____, not simply busy work.

That means . . .

1. You have a clear-cut objective.

2. You have taken time to prepare.

As you prepare, bear in mind that . . .

3. People come into class with different sets of abilities.

4. We must put our hooks into the area of their interest.

B. Good assignments must be _____.

V. Four Problems in Applying this Law

A. What happens if they come to class unprepared?

Two suggestions:

1. Do the assignment in _____.

2. Tap their _____.

Law 7

Thought Joggers

"Does it ever disturb you that there are people in your class, in your church, who have been coming for 10, 15, 20 years and still don't know the name of the game? . . . They've been under the Word, but they haven't been in it for themselves."

Helpful Hint: Ask your questions at the front end. This tells them what they are looking for, and when they see it, it builds their confidence.

"If you come into a class convinced they are not going to participate, then don't be disappointed if they don't."

HOWARD HENDRICKS / THE 7 LAWS OF THE TEACHER

Readiness

B. What if they lack confidence?

1. "If you are a teacher, you've got to generate _____."

2. "If they have confidence in you, then your job is to take that confidence and replace it in them."

C. What if someone dominates the class?

Three options:

1. Be sure to express _____ for his contribution.

2. Ask him to do you a _____: "Help me get the others involved in the process."

3. Call on him (so he knows you do value his comments).

D. What if the person is afraid to participate?

Four suggestions:

1. "Encourage people to participate and _____ them when they do."

Encourage questions . . .

Type of Question	Appropriate Response
The Simplistic Question	Express sincere appreciation for it.
The Question You Can't Answer	Say you don't know but will find out.
The Threatening Question	Make a hero out of the questioner.

2. Graduate (i.e., slowly enlarge) the experience.

   Three steps . . .

   a. What they found in the passage for themselves

   b. Neighbor nudging

   c. Participate as a class

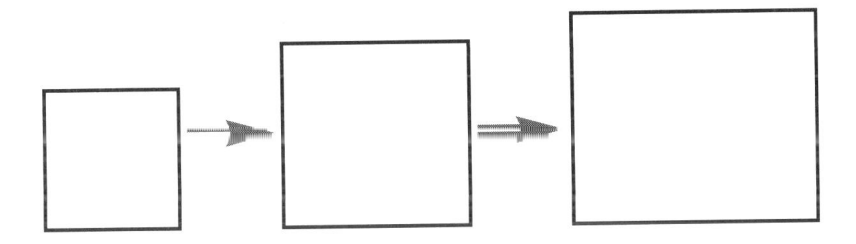

Law 7

Thought Joggers

"The only foolish question is the unasked question."

"Try to create an atmosphere in which a person who wanted to ask a question for years that he thinks is a dumb question finally is free to ask."

"By using notes, what you are doing is raising a crop of people who know how to listen intelligently."

Readiness

3. Exercise great patience.

4. Give them some _____.

   a. "Most people do not know how to take notes."

   b. Engage them in the training process—begin with basic outlines.

VI. Wrapping Up the Series

We've set before you seven basic principles of teaching . . .

The Laws of the Teacher
Teacher
Education
Activity
Communication
Heart
Encouragement
Readiness

"If you boil all of those laws down, they essentially call for a passion to _____."

> "My heart's great concern for you is that God will give you a passion that will never die. A passion to communicate. Because I have discovered that when I find a person who really gets a passion to communicate . . . he or she will go to any limit to accomplish that objective."
>
> —*Dr. Howard G. Hendricks*

Law 7

Thought Joggers

"An elderly woman taught 13 junior high boys. Today there are 84 young men in the ministry, all the product of that one woman . . . because of her passion to communicate."

HOWARD HENDRICKS / THE 7 LAWS OF THE TEACHER

Let's Talk About It

1. List three or four questions that could be used in your class to generate interest in the parable of the prodigal son (Luke 15:11-32). Discuss these with others in the group. _____

2. Within your small group, discuss appropriate readiness activities that can help prepare one of the groups below for a lesson on the feeding of the 5,000 (Luke 9:12-17):
   - older youth in Sunday school
   - men's ministry
   - women's group at fall retreat
   - afternoon Bible study group of "Super Seniors"

3. A fundamental element of master teaching is the ability to formulate thought-provoking questions. Read the questions, then rewrite each in a way that would stimulate your class to think and respond. A sample is done for you.
   Example: What country was the Good Samaritan from?
   Restated: Why do you think it was significant that the Good Samaritan was from the country of Samaria?

   A. In the parable of the seeds and the sower (Matthew 13:3-9), what kind of rocks did the seeds fall on?
   Restated: _____

   B. Mark 4:35-41 tells how Jesus calmed the storm on the sea. How big was the boat Jesus and the disciples were in?
   Restated: _____

   C. Ephesians 6:10-17 describes the armor of God that we are to wear. Won't that be awfully heavy?
   Restated: _____

Copyright © 1988, 2010 by Walk Thru the Bible Ministries, Inc. All rights reserved.

LAW 7 / THE LAW OF READINESS

How Am I Doing?

"Be prepared," the famous Boy Scout motto, echoes the words of 2 Timothy 4:2, as Paul charged Timothy: "Preach the word! Be ready in season and out of season. Convince, rebuke, exhort, with all longsuffering and teaching." On the lines below, list the tasks we are to do according to that verse, then check the description that describes you best.

	I am doing	I need to do more	I need to start doing
Preach	☐	☐	☐
_____	☐	☐	☐
_____	☐	☐	☐
_____	☐	☐	☐
_____	☐	☐	☐
_____	☐	☐	☐
_____	☐	☐	☐
_____	☐	☐	☐
_____	☐	☐	☐
_____	☐	☐	☐

Law 7

Let's Take Action

Because I am committed to following the example of Jesus Christ, the Master Teacher, I will do my best to be ready to fulfill my privilege and responsibility as a teacher. Therefore, I will do the following things before my next teaching opportunity:

_____ thoroughly prepare myself for the lesson with planned Bible study

_____ define clear-cut objectives for the lesson

_____ plan the learning activities I will use in the lesson

_____ pray daily for each member of my class

_____ write at least three or four thought-provoking questions that will generate class discussion

_____ prepare written notes to guide my teaching

On Your Own

Here are some suggestions on the use of questions in teaching:

• Prepare questions to be answered

    (a) in class
    (b) by selected readings
    (c) in writing
    (d) by experience

• Give questions based on previous classes as foundation for next class

• Have students prepare a list of personal questions about a topic or passage

• Have students prepare a series of questions that could be asked on a "final examination" of a subject

As you prepare for your next teaching session, incorporate one (or more) of the above suggestions in to your teaching plan.

LAW 7 / THE LAW OF READINESS

Notes Answer Key

Law 1
The Law of the Teacher
I.	growing
III.A.1.	learner
III.A.2.	possess
III.B.1.	arrived
III.B.2.	live
III.B.3.	satisfaction
III.B.5	humble
III.C.1.	communication/form
III.C.2.	method
IV.A.	leaders
IV.A.3.	personal
IV.B.2.	Pray
IV.C.1.	evaluated
IV.C.2.	better
IV.C.4.	in

Law 2
The Law of Education
I.A.	self-activities
I.B.	ignition/steering
I.C.	Investigator/Discoverer/Player
II.A.	time
II.B.1.	beginning
II.B.2.	discouraged
II.B.3.	older
II.B.4.	weak or disadvantaged
II.C.	interest
II.D.	resource
III.A.	think
III.A.2.	response

III.B.	learn
III.B.1.	process
III.B.2.	logical
III.B.3.	discovery
III.C.	work
IV.A.	read
IV.B.	write
IV.C.	listen
IV.D.	speak

Law 3
The Law of Activity
I.	involvement
I.C.	involvement
I.D.	understand
I.E.1.	10
I.E.2.	50
I.E.3.	90
II.A.	dictatorship
II.B.	application
II.C.	purpose
II.D.	process
II.D.1.	limitations
II.D.2.	no
II.E.	realistic
II.F.	solving
III.A.	product
III.B.	process/growth

Law 4
The Law of Communication
II.B.	common
III.B.1.	life

III.B.2.b.	they see/ 7/35/55	V.B.	communication	V.C.2.	favor
III.C.1.	package	V.C.	impact	V.D.1.	affirm
III.C.1.c.	windows	V.D.	struggling	V.D.2.c.	Self/Neighbor Nudging/Class
III.C.2.a.	Enunciation			V.D.4.	notes
III.C.2.b.	Voice	**Law 6**		VI.	communicate
III.C.2.c.	Gestures	**The Law of Encouragement**			
III.D.1.	individual	II.A.	motivated		
III.D.2.	environment	II.B.1.	act		
III.E.1.	4/10	II.B.2.a.	without		
III.G.	think/feel/doing	II.B.2.b.	within/outside		
III.H.2.	understand	IV.A.1.a.	Felt		
		IV.A.1.b.	Real		
Law 5		IV.A.1.b.1.	Scripture		
The Law of the Heart		IV.A.1.b.2.	experience		
I.	heart	IV.B.	accountability		
I.A.	totality	IV.C.	experience		
I.B.1.	character	Chart	Telling/Showing/ Controlled/Real-life		
I.B.2.	compassion				
I.B.3.	content	IV.D.	interpersonal		
I.C.1.	confidence	IV.E.	approval		
I.C.2.	motivation				
I.D.	causing/change/ you/they	**Law 7**			
		The Law of Readiness			
II.A.	learning	I.	prepared		
II.C.	Dying/Developing	III.A.	thinking		
III.A.	In Christ	III.B.	foundation		
III.B.1	feeling	III.C.	independent		
III.B.2.	care	IV.A.	creative		
IV.A.	right now	IV.B.	thought-provoking		
IV.B.	obedience	V.A.1.	class		
V.A.1.	know	V.A.2.	experience		
V.A.2.	heal	V.B.1.	confidence		
		V.C.1.	appreciation		

Copyright © 1988, 2010 by Walk Thru the Bible Ministries, Inc. All rights reserved.

Transform Your Teaching!

ACSI Accredited CEU Courses

Whether you are a professional teacher, a Sunday school teacher, a parent, or a pastor, your teaching ability and effectiveness will be transformed and so will your students!

The 7 Laws of the Learner

Transform your teaching by understanding how students learn.

When you know how students learn, then you can teach so that students absorb, comprehend, and retain new information. Influence life-changing learning!

The 7 Laws of the Teacher

Learn what is needed to be a transformational teacher.

Having knowledge doesn't mean you can effectively teach and transfer that knowledge to others. Learn what is needed to teach and to teach so well that you transform learning!

Teaching With Style

Transform your students' attentiveness and your effectiveness.

The #1 complaint about teachers is that they are boring. By understanding and applying simple principles, you'll never have a student say you weren't an engaging teacher!

Acclaimed by teachers and students alike, this classic Walk Thru the Bible teaching series has equipped teachers across the globe to better understand their students, teach in a way that transforms learning, and create a love for learning.

Buy the Set and Save $50!
Also available separately

www.walkthru.org/teachingseries or 1.800.361.6131

WALK THRU THE BIBLE
TAKE A WALK. CHANGE THE WORLD.

WALK THRU THE BIBLE Resources
TAKE A WALK. CHANGE THE WORLD.

DVD CURRICULUM
***Raise Up a Child* with Phil Tuttle**
Walk Thru the Bible Classics Series
- 7 Laws of the Leader with Bruce Wilkinson
- 7 Laws of the Teacher with Howard G. Hendricks
- A Biblical Portrait of Marriage with Bruce Wilkinson
- A Heart That Makes a Home with Bruce Wilkinson
- Leading and Loving with Bruce Wilkinson
- Personal Holiness with Bruce Wilkinson

Small Group Discussion Guides Also Available

DAILY DEVOTIONALS
Magazine Format (monthly magazines with daily readings)
Tapestry – for today's Christian woman
Daily Walk – journey through the Bible in one year
Closer Walk – journey through the New Testament in one year
Indeed – a daily devotional that explores the heart of God
Youth Walk – a daily devotional for teens and college students

BIBLES AND BOOKS
- Daily Walk Bible
- Youth Walk Bible

and more

Children's Materials
Book by Book Learning System

Old and New Testament Flashcards

But is it really Bible teaching?

...Absolutely!

LIVE EVENTS - Informative and fun!
Schedule a live event for your church or organization.
20 million people from 85 countries have attended our life changing events!
- Walk Thru the Old Testament
- Walk Thru the New Testament
- Kids in the Book Old Testament
- Kids in the Book New Testament
- Effective Parenting in a Defective World
- Raise Up a Child
- Understanding the Love of Your Life
- A Biblical Portrait of Marriage
- 7 Laws of the Learner
- 7 Laws of the Teacher
- Solving the People Puzzle

Learn more at www.walkthru.org or call 1.800.361.6131

Notes

Notes